PUFFIN BOOKS
LET'S DO THIS TOGETHER

Vineeta Kanoria has been a preschool educator for over 20 years. She also set up the Early Intervention Centre at Ummeed Child Development Center for children with special needs. She enjoys helping children and parents discover the joys of maths at an early age.

Lubaina Bandukwala has been in children's publishing as a writer, editor and festival curator for a decade. She founded the Peek A Book Literature Festival for children, which is now in its fourth year. She does all this so that she can read all the books she wants anytime she pleases and say she's working.

PRAISE FOR THE BOOK

'The idea of having a book of stories on math is one of the coolest, smartest ways of teaching this dreaded subject to kids and parents alike.'—Gopika Kapoor, author of *Spiritual Parenting*

'The snappy stories and delightful illustrations enable children to develop a love for math at an early age . . . We need more books like these!'—Preeti Vyas, author of *The Adventures of Woka Chimni*

'Parents will definitely enjoy reading these stories to their children, who in turn, will enjoy working out the small math problems thrown in. In fact, the children wouldn't even realise that they are being made to work out sums.'—Lekha Merchant, head teacher, Saifee-Eide-Zahabi Nursery School

MATHS STORIES TO SOLVE

# Let's do this Together

Lubaina Bandukwala
Vineeta Kanoria

Illustrations by Zainab Tambawalla

PUFFIN BOOKS
An imprint of Penguin Random House

PUFFIN BOOKS

USA | Canada | UK | Ireland | Australia
New Zealand | India | South Africa | China | Singapore

Puffin Books is part of the Penguin Random House group of companies
whose addresses can be found at global.penguinrandomhouse.com

Published by Penguin Random House India Pvt. Ltd
4th Floor, Capital Tower 1, MG Road,
Gurugram 122 002, Haryana, India

Penguin
Random House
India

First published in India by Vakils, Feffer and Simons Pvt. Ltd. 2018
Published in India in Puffin Books by Penguin Random House India 2019

ISBN 9780143448105

Typeset in Adobe Caslon Pro by Manipal Digital Systems, Manipal
Printed at Repro India Limited

www.penguin.co.in

This is a legitimate digitally printed version of the book and therefore might not
have certain extra finishing on the cover.

# Foreword

This book has come into being for several reasons:

For Rehaan, my *jaan*. Because he is now four—an age when he can understand how cool maths is.

For maths. For making it fun, so that no one can frighten your child silly any more with the idea of it. At this level, maths is concrete; yet, it nudges your child to be flexible and automatic with numbers.

For you, dear parents. For story time and helping you develop a deeper bond with your child.

I have been a teacher and special educator for nearly three decades now. Along with my colleague Mala Chadha, I conduct workshops for parents and teachers and introduce them to interesting ways to teach reading, writing and maths. Being special educators, we structure our programmes systematically, but we also take 'fun' very seriously. Children must learn through games and stories, in a manner that they don't realise they are being taught—that has been our mantra.

So, when we came across a book by Peggy Kaye, which explains how a student was coaxed into carrying out mathematical operations while listening to stories—we were delighted. This ingenious idea, we felt, deserved a dedicated book. And then the magical Lubaina stepped into the scene and waved her wand and before I knew it, this book was in my hand. Ever grateful for her presence and talent.

May these storytelling sessions create wonderful memories for you and your child! And if the stories succeed in unleashing your imagination and creativity, or if you have any feedback, then do write in to us with your experiences at letsditmaths@gmail.com. We would love to hear from you.

Vineeta Kanoria,
Mumbai 2018

# How to Read This Book: A Note for Parents

Before you embark on this arithmetic ride, here are a few tips:

- Read through the stories first before reading them aloud to your child. This way, you will be able to read fluently and hold your child's attention.
- The stories are divided into three sections— **Easy Peasy**, **Mostly Easy**, and **Not So Easy**— with increasing levels of complexity. Begin according to your kid's level, moving slowly to the more challenging stories.

- Do the maths with them—help them use their fingers, everyday objects or even a paper and a pencil for this.
- Add drama, use fun voices and intonations. Read in a relaxed manner. It's not a test; it's a story! Make it joyful for the child.

# CUT A FRUIT, SECTION A VEGETABLE AND TAKE A PEEK AT NATURE'S MATHS.

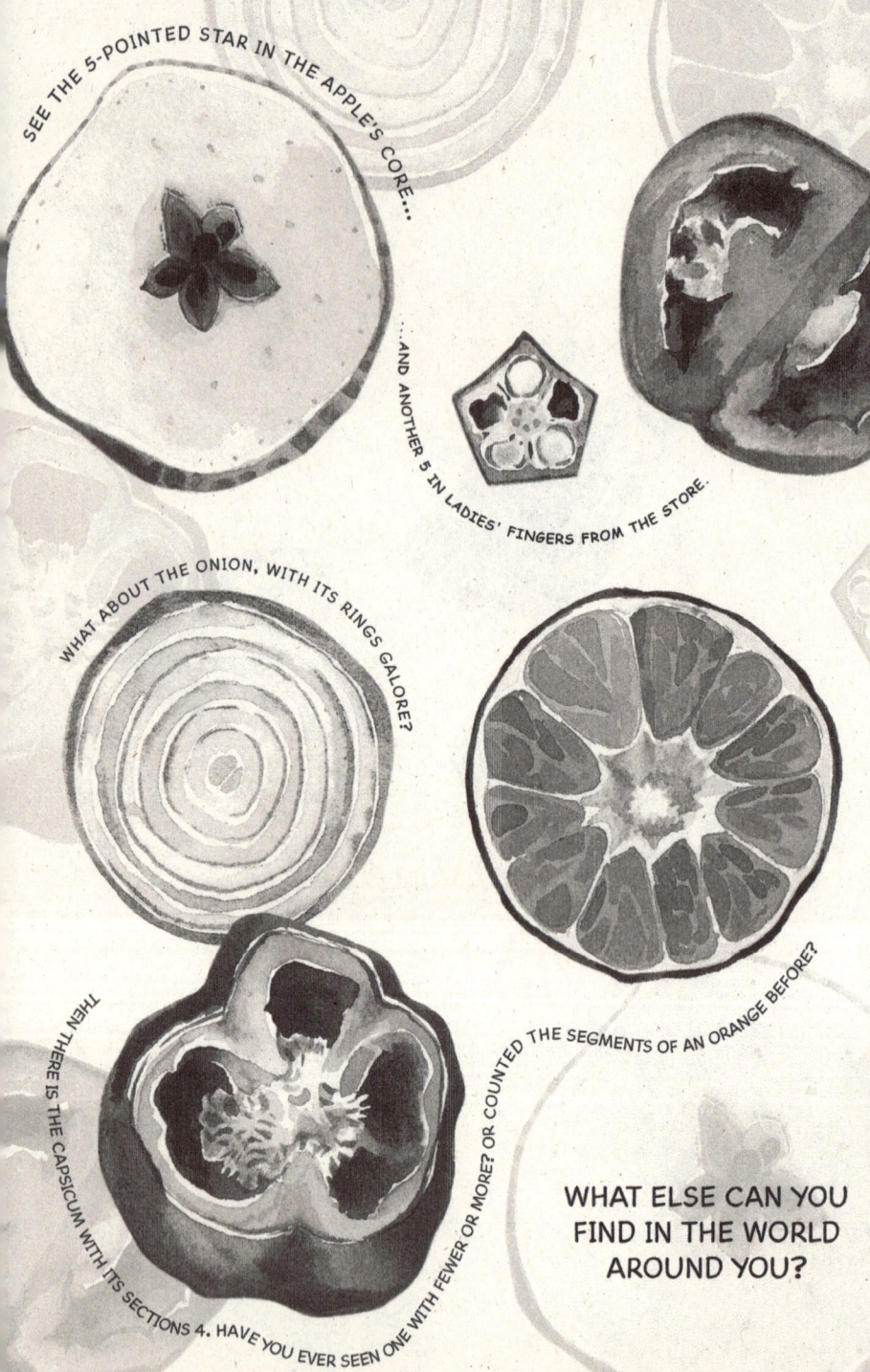

SEE THE 5-POINTED STAR IN THE APPLE'S CORE...

...AND ANOTHER 5 IN LADIES' FINGERS FROM THE STORE.

WHAT ABOUT THE ONION, WITH ITS RINGS GALORE?

THEN THERE IS THE CAPSICUM WITH ITS SECTIONS 4. HAVE YOU EVER SEEN ONE WITH FEWER OR MORE? OR COUNTED THE SEGMENTS OF AN ORANGE BEFORE?

## WHAT ELSE CAN YOU FIND IN THE WORLD AROUND YOU?

# Easy-Peasy

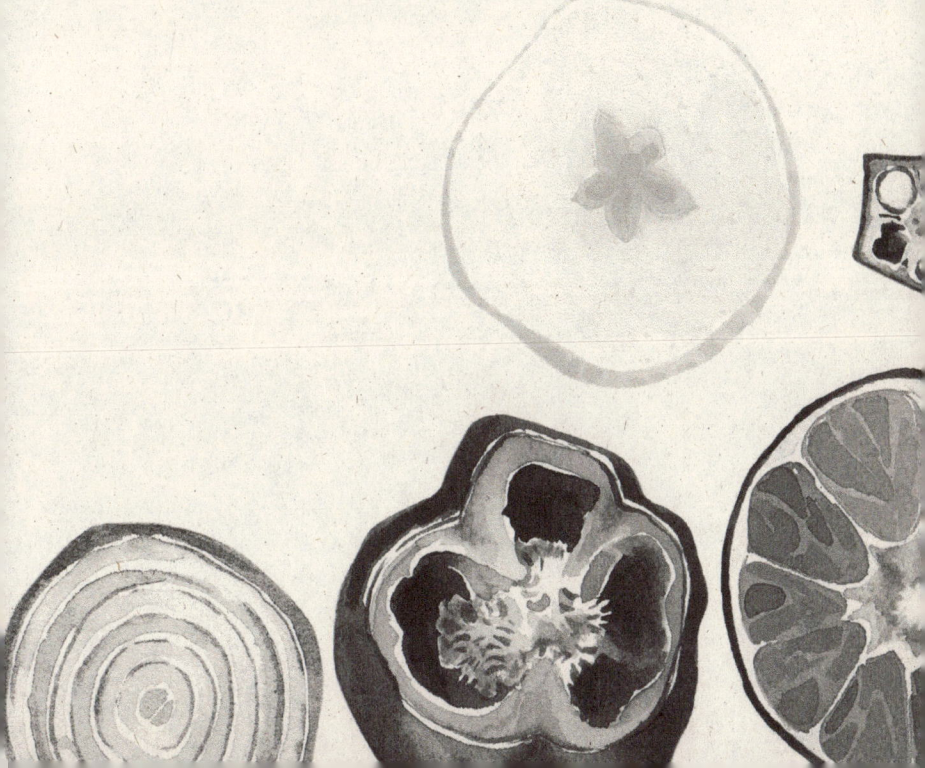

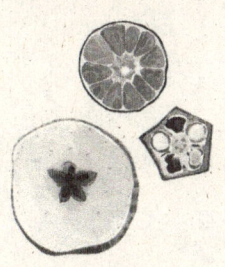

# Story Time!

Rehaan's mom would read him a bedtime story every night. He loved to listen to his favourite stories again and again. Hearing the same words in her special 'story voice' made him feel safe and comfortable. But his mom couldn't understand that and read the story only once! MOMS!

One night, Rehaan wasn't sleepy at all, and he wanted to hear more than 1 story. His mom had just finished telling him the story of *The Three Little Pigs*. He just loved the part where the wolf huffed and puffed and tried to blow the brick house down. His mom, he had to admit, played the role of the wolf really well. He kept wondering how he could convince his mom to tell him more than 1 story.

Just as she was about to switch off the light, Rehaan made a sad face.

'You know I fell down today? And now my leg is really hurting. Maybe I'll feel better if you tell me another story,' he said.

His mom smiled and read him the story of *The Three Billy Goats Gruff*.

Rehaan was still wide awake when the story ended. So he said, 'Mom, I think that *Goldilocks and the Three Bears* would feel really disappointed if their story wasn't told.' Smart little Rehaan, eh? His mother had to give in!

How many stories did he get his mother to tell him that night?

# Pizza Party

Yay! It's pizza-making day. Every Saturday, Zara and Sara help their dad make pizzas. Today, they are making a mixed-cheese pizza and a paneer pizza.

Dad asks Zara to bring out the yellow cheese, pizza cheese and cheddar cheese from the fridge. How many types of cheese is Zara going to get from the fridge?

He then asks Sara to bring him the paneer and the tomato sauce. How many ingredients will Sara get from the fridge?

Dad spreads the sauce on the pizzas. Zara covers 2 of the pizzas with grated cheese. Sara covers 3 more with crumbled paneer. Then they pop these into the oven and watch eagerly as the pizzas bake and the cheese bubbles and melts into golden gooeyness. How many pizzas have they made in all?

# Funny, Funny Monkey

'Cheeee!' came a sound from somewhere over my head. I was eating a banana as I walked in the park with Dad. I looked up.

'Cheeee!'

It was the screeching of a tiny monkey that was blinking down at me, with a mischievous look in its eyes. Suddenly, it swooped down and snatched the banana from my hand. 'Ahhh!' I screamed as I leapt back in fright! The naughty creature! It ran back up the tree and waved my fruit at me.

I saw 2 more come down the trees towards me and stand on my left. 'Don't worry,' said Dad, 'if you don't have any food, they won't bother you.' As he said this, yet another monkey swooped down from the tree to my right and plucked the hat from Dad's head!

'Ahhh!' yelled Dad. We laughed till our stomachs hurt.

Later, when I was telling my mom about this, I couldn't remember how many monkeys there had been in all. Can you help me?

PISTA SHELLS ARE FUN TO COUNT.

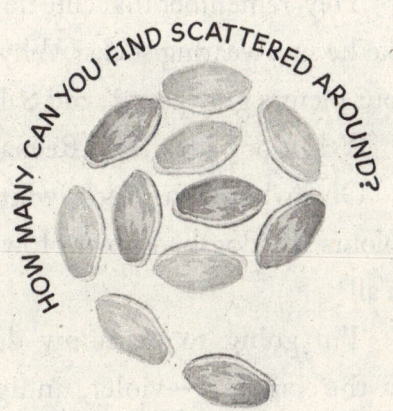

HOW MANY CAN YOU FIND SCATTERED AROUND?

# Colour, Colour, Which Colour?

Reena drew a picture of a dog. She wanted to colour him brown and black. How many colours would the dog in the picture have?

Rahul looked at the drawing and said, 'I think he should have a white ear.' Reena agreed. How many colours would the drawing have now?

'Hey, remember that cute dog on the street who looked like he was wearing socks? Why don't you give the dog in your picture grey paws?' said Sahil.

'Yes! Good idea,' said Reena.

Oh my! Brown, black, white and grey, what a lot of colours the dog had now! How many colours were there in all?

'I'm going to paint my dog using all the colours of the rainbow—violet, indigo, blue, green, yellow, orange and red!' exclaimed Nyra, who had also drawn a dog. How many colours is Nyra going to use to colour the dog?

# Drip Drop

Big black clouds gathered outside Shirin's window. Shirin was too busy playing with her building blocks, so she didn't notice them at first. But when it began to rain, the little girl ran to her window. First, a few drops fell on her windowpane with a *plop, plop, plop*. How many drops had fallen on Shirin's window? Then came 5 more. How many drops had fallen there in all?

Then the drops fell so fast—*plop, plop, plop, plop*—that she couldn't count them any more! After some time, the rain stopped. She saw 5 pretty drops clinging to the window pane, shining bright as diamonds. After a while, 2 of these became really thin streams and slipped away. How many raindrops remained on the glass?

# Birthday Presents

The best part about a birthday party is, of course, the presents! Rahima couldn't wait to see them. So, as soon as all her friends had gone home, she said, 'Mom, let's open my presents!'

'Yes, mine too!' agreed her twin brother, Siraj. After all, it was his birthday as well!

'Yay, a sand art kit!' Rahima squealed, unwrapping the first gift. As she opened a few more, she found 2 more such kits. How many of these did Rahima get?

Meanwhile, Siraj too had torn open his gifts. And guess what? He too had received 3 sand art kits! Between them, how many sand art kits did the twins have?

Then Rahima counted the puzzle books that had been gifted to her. There were 4 of those. Siraj found that he had received 4 puzzle books as well! In all, how many puzzle books did they get?

# Oh, You're Impossible!

Louis, a waiter at a fancy French restaurant, was terribly clumsy. Nearly every night, he would splash soup on a diner or drop bread rolls on another. But the things that he dropped most often were plates!

One Friday, at lunchtime, he dropped 2 plates and at dinner time, 4 more slipped from his hands. How many plates did he drop on Friday?

'Oh, you're impossible!' said his boss, M Armand.

On Saturday, at lunchtime, Louis, once again, dropped 2 plates, and at dinner time, 7 more fell. How many plates did he drop on Saturday?

'Argh! you're impossible!' exclaimed his boss, M Armand.

Then he dropped 2 plates during lunch hour on Sunday and at dinner, 8 more. How many plates did he drop on Sunday?

'Harrumph! You're impossible!' said his boss, M Armand.

On Monday, he tried to be extra careful. He did not drop any plates at lunchtime. And you know what? He did not drop a single plate at dinner time either!

'No broken plates?' asked a shocked M Armand. 'What? That's impossible!'

# All Arms and Legs

Mahnaaz, like many of us, had 2 legs. But it got a bit boring sometimes. So she pretended to have 2 more legs—that way, she could be a dog, cat or even a leopard! How many legs did she pretend to have in all to become a leopard?

Sometimes, she decided to give herself 2 more legs and 2 more arms—that way she could be a spider and crawl up the walls and hang upside down from the ceiling! How many limbs (arms and legs together) did she pretend to have to become a spider?

Then, one night, as she lay on her bed, the full moon shone bright blue in the sky and the curtains in her window swayed in the breeze. It all seemed a bit scary. But, instead of running to her mama's room, she gave herself 3 more arms and 8 more legs. So how many arms and how many legs did Mahnaaz think she had?

And why did these extra arms and legs make her feel better? That's because she was pretending to be an alien with many arms and legs. Nothing could scare her now!

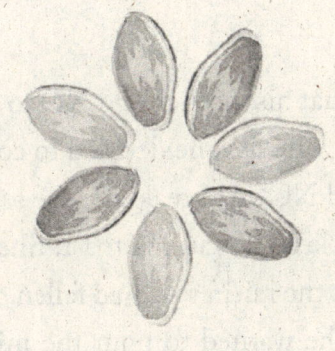

# No!

Vivaan felt that his mother said NO to him ALL THE TIME! So, one day, he decided to count the number of times she said NO. At breakfast, she said NO when he wanted to use a knife to cut his toast. She said NO when he wanted to eat the raisin that had fallen on the floor. She said NO when he wanted to pour the milk from the jug into his glass. When he wanted to eat the banana whole, she stopped him by saying NO again. How many times did Vivaan's mother say no at breakfast?

Later, when she took Vivaan to play in the park, he asked her if he could jump off the slide. She said NO. She also said NO when he wanted to take the blue spade that belonged to another child. How many times did his mother say no in the park?

When they returned from the park, it was bath time. Vivaan wanted to splash about and wet the bathroom floor, and his mother said NO. Then he wanted to squash the soap, she said NO. She said NO again when he wanted to stay under the shower for some more time. How many times did she say no at bath time?

So, if we count the number of times Vivaan's mother said no at breakfast, at the park and as he had his bath, how many times did she say NO in the entire day?

# Monsters Under My Bed

Every night, after mom has turned off the lights, left my room and shut the door behind her, my monster friends come out from under my bed for a picnic. I set out a red checked cloth with glasses, plates and clay cupcakes for 8 monsters. All of them are purple with bright green ears. They speak in French. I don't know French, but strangely, we can talk to and understand each other.

Last night, after mom had tucked me in, I jumped out of bed, laid out the picnic cloth, and called out to my friends. One by one they crept out from under my bed. When all 8 were out, I said, 'Let's begin our party!' But Goofunk, the biggest of them all, said, 'Wait, we have some more friends coming.' And much to my surprise, 2 more monsters came out. These were not purple but bright yellow with scarlet stars on them! But they were

just as nice and friendly as my other monster buddies, so I set out 2 more plates for them.

How many monsters sat down to share a picnic last night?

I offered them milkshake and orange juice. The juice was chosen by 6 of the monsters. How many preferred the milkshake?

# Happy Families

Rahul hated family gatherings. Mom and Dad expected him to know the names of ALL the relatives there! What's more, his sister always knew everyone's names and was such a show off!

'Rahul, please try and remember the names of your aunts and uncles this time!' said his dad.

As soon as he walked in, Shalu Aunty, Tia Didi and Reena Bua gave him big smacking kisses on his cheeks—which irritated him so very much! How many people kissed him?

Rajesh Kaka pinched his cheeks, which irritated him even more! How many people pinched his cheeks?

And Vivek Uncle, Radha Aunty, Indra Aunty and Ram Bhaiya exclaimed, 'How big you have grown!'—as if any child would grow small! How many relatives told him that he had grown so big?

Suddenly, Rahul had an idea! He would use their irritating habits to remember their names—the ones who kissed his cheek, the cheek pinchers and the 'how-big-you-are' commenters. He would never forget their names now!

# Vishal's New Friends

Vishal was sad, angry and fed up. He had moved into a new home, but he had no new friends. In his old building, he played *dhappa* with Gia and Ayesha. And he played a card game with Sia, Harvesh and Binny. How many friends did he play with in his old building?

Here he was now, playing alone in the park. A little black puppy kept following him around. Vishal threw his red ball near the pup to shoo it away, careful enough not to hurt it. 'Go away,' he said. The ball rolled away and the puppy ran after it.

Within seconds, the puppy came back. In his mouth, he was carrying a green ball and a yellow one too. Vishal was annoyed! 'Hey, where is my red ball?' he asked the pup sternly.

The puppy dived back into the bushes. This time, he came back with a pink ball and a blue ball. How many balls did the puppy get for Vishal?

'Red ball!' Vishal pointed in the opposite direction again. The puppy ran off and finally brought back the boy's red ball.

'Hey, where's my yellow ball?' a boy who was walking through the bushes asked aloud. Three more children who were looking for their lost balls came towards Vishal and the pup. 'Hello,' said one of the boys, 'Are you new here? Would you like to play with us?' Vishal was thrilled. He now had new friends to play with. How many new friends did he now have? (Don't forget the pup!)

# The Chicken and the Egg

A farmer had bought 3 fluffy yellow chicks for his farm. They grew into a brown hen, a white hen and a speckled hen. Every day, the farmer's boy would check if they had laid any eggs. And every day, he would find an empty nest.

One day, several months later, when the boy went to check, he was delighted! The brown hen, the white hen and the speckled hen had laid 2 eggs each. How many eggs did the farmer's boy collect that day?

The boy was so excited that he dropped an egg by mistake on his way back to the farmhouse. How many eggs did he have left?

The farmer's wife had a recipe for a cake that needed 2 eggs. After she took 2 eggs from her son, how many remained?

The farmer's daughter wanted to have 1 boiled egg and her brother wanted 2 boiled eggs. How many eggs did the mother boil for her children? Were there any eggs left after that?

# The Front Seat

'I will sit in the seat next to the driver!' said Sachi.
'No! I will!' replied Nisha.

Thus, a fight broke out as soon as both the girls got on to the school bus—this happened every day.

Bus Didi had had enough. 'Stop it, both of you!'

'From next week, on Mondays, Wednesdays and Fridays, Sachi will sit in front. And on Tuesdays, Thursdays and Saturdays, Nisha will take the front seat. Is that clear?' she asked.

For how many days in a week would each of them sit in the front seat? Do you think each got an equal chance?

# Sandcastles

Teenu loved making sandcastles on the beach. And he loved to make them close to the water, because when he dug a moat around the castles, the waves filled them with water naturally.

One day, Teenu's family decided to spend their afternoon at the beach. Mom and Dad settled on the beach chairs and Minnie took off to find shells. Teenu set out to make his castles. First, he made a tall one with a deep moat. Then he made another, squat and square. The next one was shaped like a star. After that, he made 2 smaller ones. How many castles did he make in all?

'Teenu, come here, the tide is rising!' Mom called out. Teenu looked towards the sea. While he had been busy with his other castles, the water had risen—half of his tall castle had already drowned! Then a big wave rushed in and washed it away entirely. Oh no! How many castles remained?

Another big wave came in and swooshed over the square and the star-like ones. How many castles were left now?

Teenu looked at the remaining castles. *I'm glad these are higher on the beach*, he thought. *The waves can't get them!* But as he bent down to pick up his bucket and spade, he saw 2 stray dogs jump on to the castles.

The boy was so angry, he felt like crying! 'Uff, you silly dogs,' he said, stamping his foot. The dog with a black splotch around one eye—which made him look like a pirate—looked at Teenu and wagged his tail gently. *I like this castle*, he seemed to say. And Teenu couldn't help but smile. There's plenty of sand to make more castles, after all. So Teenu got to work again. This time, he made them far away from the big waves.

# The Rose Garden

It was the month of March. Mr Mehta stood proudly in the middle of his rose garden. His prize-winning roses were in full bloom. His favourite, though, was a special variety called Purple Rain. Mr Mehta was careful enough not to let a single caterpillar or insect bother his plants. But, that morning, Mr Mehta saw 2 caterpillars happily eating the leaves of Purple Rain. 'Argh!' he cried in horror. Carefully picking the caterpillars off the plant, he placed them outside the fence surrounding his garden.

The next day, to his dismay, he found 2 new caterpillars on Purple Rain, 3 caterpillars among the Ruby Red rose bushes and 5 among the Pink Blush rose bushes. How many caterpillars did Mr Mehta find in the garden that day? He sprayed organic pesticide on his roses and went away thinking that that was the end of the caterpillars.

A few days later, as he was walking through his garden, he saw 4 brown moths and 8 brown grey moths flying over his rose bushes. If each moth had been a caterpillar, then how many caterpillars had still been hiding in Mr Mehta's garden?

# Double or Quits

Batul and Neelu were best friends. Batul had a fairy godmother and for every wish that she granted Batul, Batul wanted double, so that it could be shared with Neelu.

'Oh no, I want 2!' Batul cried out loud.

The fairy godmother sighed.

In vain, the fairy godmother tried to explain to Batul that she was not supposed to grant wishes to anyone but her chosen child. In fact, she could well lose her wish-making license from the Fairy Government! But no, Batul was quite stubborn about it.

'Batul, here's your wish for 2 red markers,' his fairy godmother would say.

'I need double,' said Batul.

How many markers did her fairy godmother have to present?

'Okay, here are the 7 doughnuts you wished for.'

'I need double,' insisted Batul.

How many doughnuts did Batul need?

'I've got 12 apples for you.'

'I need double,' frowned Batul.

How many apples did Batul need?

Her fairy godmother was quite fed up and decided she must do something about this. One sunny day, Batul wished for rain. The fairy godmother decided to give her double. It rained and rained and Batul got so wet, she caught a horrible cold. When she wished it to get sunny again, her fairy godmother turned up the heat to double, until Batul could barely walk for the heat.

'Stop, stop!' Batul cried. 'I get your point, I don't want double of anything. I will just share what I get with Neelu.' Her fairy godmother was delighted. Her plan had worked.

SUCH BEAUTIFUL PATTERNS YOU WILL SEE, IF ONLY YOU LOOK AT THE LEAVES OF A PLANT, SHRUB OR TREE!

IN SOME YOU WILL SPY SYMMETRY—WHERE THE LEFT SIDE MATCHES THE RIGHT.

IN OTHERS YOU WILL SEE THE FIBONACCI—A SPIRAL PATTERN OF GROWTH—IN WHICH NATURE TAKES GREAT DELIGHT.

CAN YOU FIND TESSELLATIONS (REPEATING PATTERNS)?

# Mostly Easy

# Musical Chairs

'It's time to play musical chairs!'

'Yay!' yelled the children. Cyrus' birthday parties were always so much fun!

There were 10 children, so 10 chairs were first placed in a row.

The music started and the children ran around the row of chairs. When it stopped, all of them found a chair and sat down immediately!

Then before the music started again, Cyrus' mom took away 1 chair. How many children could sit the next time the music stopped? How many would get out?

After ten minutes, 5 children were still in the game. How many were out?

# Circus! Circus!

Rehaan went to the circus with his mother. He saw that the juggler had 1 ball in each hand and 8 in the air. How many balls was he juggling with?

Just then, the lion let out a big roar. The balls began to fall from the frightened juggler's hands, but he managed to catch 4 of them. How many balls fell down?

When the elephant saw some of the balls on the floor, he decided to kick them right out of the circus tent. And so, 3 balls flew out of the tent before the juggler could stop the elephant. How many balls did the elephant miss?

The juggler was upset. How many balls did he have left in total, including the ones on the floor?

The next day, the juggler went to the shop and bought 3 new balls to complete his set. He was now ready to perform his juggling act again.

# Fruit Salad Surprise

It was Saturday and Adi's friend Vanya came over to play. They decided to surprise Adi's father with a fruit salad. First, they made a list of the fruits they would use. Adi wanted to put in an orange, some strawberries and grapes. Vanya said she wanted to add an apple and some bananas. How many kinds of fruit would their salad have in all?

Vanya took 3 bananas and started peeling them, but the bananas were slippery and 1 fell down. Of course, they could not use that one! So how many bananas could they use?

Adi put 5 grapes in the salad bowl, but he felt that was too less—so he added 3 more. How many grapes were in the bowl in all?

There were 10 strawberries in the fruit basket. Adi was going to put them all in the salad bowl, when he saw that

3 of those were rotten. How many strawberries could he use?

Adi and Vanya then added some salt, sugar and pepper to the fruits. It was finally ready. In his excitement, Adi's father gobbled up the delicious fruit salad and forgot to share it with anyone!

A WALLET FULL OF COINS

HOW MANY CAN YOU FIND?

# Cake in your Face!

Just before the cake was cut at Shaurya's birthday party, his mom made the kids play one more game.

Renu Aunty gave each child two boxes of marbles. 'Count the marbles from both these boxes. Those children who have exactly 10 marbles altogether will get to put cake on Shaurya's face!'

The children giggled and laughed as they reached excitedly for the boxes. *I hope it's me*, every kid thought secretly!

Naina got 8 marbles in one box and 3 in the other.

Shamin got 6 marbles in one box and 4 in the other.

Mukul got 3 marbles in one box and 8 in the other.

Rakesh got 3 marbles in one box and 7 in another.

Satya got 9 marbles in one box and 1 in the other.

Who got to put cake on Shaurya's face?

# Waiting for Cousins

Shirin's cousins were coming from the USA, and she couldn't wait to see them. They would reach here in 10 more hours. Oh, but time passed by so slowly.

'Shirin, stop fidgeting! Come and help me get the guest room ready,' her mom said. So she helped to change the sheets and place a new soap and shampoo in the bathroom, for her cousins to use. They finished all the work in 2 hours. How much time is left for her cousins to arrive?

'Why don't you go play with your friends?' said her mom. So Shirin went off to her friend Ayesha's house. They watched videos of DIY crafts online and made lots of fun stuff for 4 more hours. But when she went back home, she realised that there was still so much time left. How many hours more would Shirin have to wait?

She then helped her mom bake a banana and walnut cake and make *sev puri*, which her cousins loved. This took them 2 hours. How much longer will her cousins take to arrive?

# Mamma, When Will It Be Eid?

'Mamma, when will it be Eid?' six-year-old Zainab asked.

'When we see the new moon in the sky,' replied her mom.

'When will there be a new moon in the sky?' the girl asked.

'You will see a full moon in the sky 15 days from today. And 15 days after that, you will see the new moon,' her mom explained.

In how many days from today will Zainab see the new moon?

# Under the Sea

Have you ever snorkelled around a coral reef? I have. I wore a mask with a long tube and sat in a boat that took me to the coral reef. Once we got there, I slipped into the water from the boat and stuck my head underwater.

Suddenly, I was in a different world. There was no sound in this world. And the light was bluish green. The world bobbed and gently swayed. And right before my eyes, a school of yellow-and-black striped fish darted past. There were 10 of them. Then 10 more came! How many yellow-and-black fish did I see?

And upon a cloud of bubbles rose 10 tiny seahorses. Right behind them were 10 beautiful angelfish. How many seahorses and angelfish had I seen altogether?

Down in the shadows, I saw an octopus resting next to a sea urchin. A small reef shark swam around lazily. I spied

an eel slipping into the corals. How many sea creatures had I seen in the shadows?

It was then time to go back to my world. And I must say that although my head returned to sunshine, my heart remained in the blue-green waters. With the striped fish and the octopus, the seahorses and the angelfish! I hope I can go back there again soon.

# Flamingo Watch

The children looked out of their window. Far out on the mudflats, by the river, was a patch of pink. Sia picked up her binoculars and looked through them. 'I can see 28 flamingos today,' she said. Samina wrote down the date and the number.

Every year during winter, the children waited for the flamingos to come from their home in the Rann of Kutch in Gujarat. The children, who had been waiting for the birds eagerly this year too, delightedly watched the birds feeding on some algae and small fish in the shallows.

A few days later, the girls looked through the binoculars again. 'I can find only 19 today,' Samina said. How many flamingos had flown away?

Two more days later, they decided to count the flamingos again.

'That's 6 less than the last time,' sighed Sia.

'Oh no!' exclaimed Samina.

How many flamingos were left now?

And on the very next day, when the girls checked, all of them were gone! Summer had officially begun.

# Birdwatching

Little sparrows hopped on to the balcony and pecked at the seeds that were in the bird feed. There were 10 of them. Soon, 10 more flew in and sat on the railing and cocked their little heads this way and that. And when it appeared safe, they hopped on to the seeds as well. How many sparrows were now eating from the feeder?

Perhaps sparrows have newspapers of their own, because the news of the seeds spread quickly, and 10 more landed on the balcony, fluttering their wings and cheeping noisily. How many sparrows were on the balcony now?

Then the sparrows had an unexpected visitor—a crow. As the crow hopped through the group of sparrows, its large wings outstretched, many of the sparrows stepped back in fright. Within minutes, 10 sparrows flew away. How many sparrows were now left?

And then, another crow came. Of course, as soon as the second crow came, yet another batch of 10 sparrows flew away. How many sparrows were left on the balcony now?

# The Most Popular Snack Box

Xavier's snack box was popular amongst his friends. His lunch box always contained extras from the bakery that his parents owned. Everyone was pleased with Xavier's tiffin, except Xavier himself!

On Monday, he had brought 3 jam tarts. He had barely opened it when Roshan, Hitaxshi and Sahil came up to his desk. How many friends came to share his tiffin? If they took 1 tart each, would there be any left for Xavier?

On Tuesday, Xavier's tiffin was a treat of 4 chocolate brownies. He gave 1 to Sara for helping him with his maths classwork. Roshan, Hitaxshi and Sahil showed up again, and Xavier had to give a brownie to each of his 3 friends. Did he have a brownie left for himself?

Thursday was a difficult day. His box had 1 big pizza! When his 3 friends came along, he realised that he would have to cut the pizza into pieces. How many pizza pieces would he need for his friends and himself so that they would all have 2 pieces each?

On Friday, he finally got it right. He had, in his lunch box, 1 curry puff for himself, 1 for Sara (because she had helped him with maths again), and 1 each for Roshan, Hitaxshi and Sahil. How many curry puffs had he carried to school that day?

# A Special Party

Summer holidays had begun and the kids in Taj Mahal Towers were waiting for a special invitation—an invitation from Rajini's Dadi. And on 2 May, Suraiya, Rajiv, Dilkhush and Aryan were invited to Rajini's house to help make this year's mango pickle! How many children were going to help Dadi make pickle?

'First things first,' said Dadi. 'Wash your hands!'

'Yes, Dadi!' the children chorused.

'Now the 3 of you, carefully take 10 mangoes each out of the basket,' she then said.

How many mangoes in all were going to be pickled?

'Cut each mango into 6 pieces. Careful! The knives are very sharp!' How many pieces of mango in all were going into the pickle?

'Now the rest of you will need to measure out the spices,' continued Dadi.

How many children were going to measure out the spices?

Then Dadi mixed the oil, spices, salt and mangoes together and filled several jars with this mixture. There were 2 jars for Rajini's home, 1 each for her friends and 2 extra jars. How many jars of pickle did they make in all?

# Strong, Stronger, Strongest

Whenever Saloni and her friends Alina and Dhruva went to the mall, they had a competition to show off who amongst them was the strongest on the high striker.

The high striker is a game where the player strikes a small platform, as hard as possible, with a hammer. This makes a ball shoot up on a tall scale attached to this platform. The ball stops at a number to indicate the level of strength—the weakest strike stops at number 1 and the strongest at number 10.

Dhruva's hit usually made the ball go up to Level 5. Saloni generally managed to strike hard enough to get the ball to reach Level 4, while Alina managed to touch Level 6. How many levels stronger than Saloni was she?

That day, Saloni was determined to win this game. She decided to go last. As usual, Alina managed Level 6 and Dhruva level 5. Then Saloni took the hammer, took a deep breath, and hit hard. And the ball shot up to Level 7! Did she win the competition this time?

# Concert Time

Aadil, Tarini and Parini each played the piano. Apart from that, Tarini also played the violin, Parini played the flute and Aadil played the violin and the trumpet too.

How many children played only 1 musical instrument?

The school band was looking for children who played 2 musical instruments to join them for a special concert. Who could join the band?

As the bandleader, the school wanted a child who could play 3 instruments. Who will be chosen as the bandleader?

# Three Buddies

Kittu, Bittu and Chuha (as they called each other) shared everything from secrets to sweets and always got up to a lot of mischief. Chuha, despite being the youngest, was the leader. Whatever he did, the other two had to match up to him, but they often failed. Once, Chuha ate 5 burgers in one go. Kittu and Bittu only managed to finish 3 each and by the end of it, they were so sick! How many more burgers than Kittu and Bittu had Chuha eaten?

Another time, Chuha rang 3 doorbells before hiding; Kittu and Bittu only managed to ring 1. What's worse, they even got caught!

Yet another time, they decided to start a paper-plane flying competition. But no one was a match for Chuha. He had finished throwing 3 paper planes around the classroom, while the other two were still making the planes.

One day, during lunch break, Chuha showed off that he could skip 50 times without stopping. Bittu tried, but managed only 44. By how many skipping rounds did Bittu fail to match up to Chuha's record?

Chuha puffed his chest out with pride and said, 'Kittu, let's see how you do in this challenge.' As Kittu skipped on and on, everyone counted, ' . . . 48, 49, 50, . . . ' Yet, Kittu didn't stop. He continued skipping all the way to 65! Did Kittu beat Chuha? By how many times?

There was a stunned silence. Then everyone started clapping and cheering—Chuha, the loudest of all. He was truly proud of his friend!

# Yuck! Peas!

Saira picked out the peas in her rice, counting slowly, '. . . 81, 82, 83, 84 . . . 90—I hate peas!'

Her mom walked into the room and saw the neat pile of peas on one side of Saira's plate. 'Excuse me, young lady, you have to finish everything. And I mean EVERYTHING on your plate, if you want a piece of gooey chocolate mud pie.'

'Ugh!' Saira looked down at the peas.

As soon as her mom went back into the kitchen to fetch something, she fed 20 peas to her cat Simba, who promptly ate them up.

How many peas did she have to eat now?

'Would you like some?' she whispered to her doll Simran and her purple unicorn Badshah. Without waiting for them to answer, she slid 10 peas on to Simran's little dish and another 10 on to Badshah's plate.

When her mom came back, how many peas did Saira have on her plate?

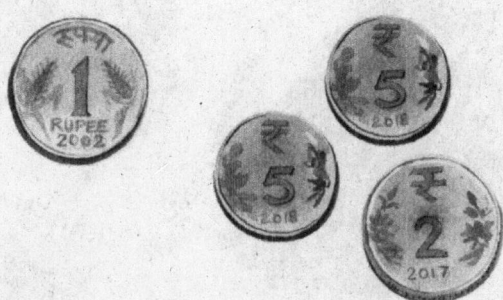

NATURE USES MATHS TO
MAKE BEAUTIFUL ART.

IN SEASHELLS YOU WILL FIND ALL KINDS OF SPIRALS. REPEATING CIRCULAR PATTERNS CREATE NAUTILUS SHELL.

AND YOU CAN SEE A CONE SHELL'S REPEATING POLYGONS VERY WELL.

'DID YOU KNOW THAT
99% OF MOLLUSC
SHELLS ARE 'DEXTRAL'
(THEY ONLY OPEN TO
THE RIGHT)?'

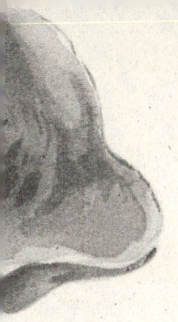

# Not That Easy

# Eenie, Meenie, Minie, Mo

Eenie, Meenie, Minie, Mo,
See those pretty boxes 4?
In one of them lies a prize
If you pick the one that's right!
Eenie, Meenie, Minie, Mo

Choose the box that totals up to 5 x 4
2, 8, 20, 9, 4, 7

Eenie, Meenie, Minie, Mo
What's inside?
Is that the prize?
No. Not yet!
In one of 4 boxes within, it lies.
Eenie, Meenie, Minie, Mo

Answer this to win the prize
Is 3 x 4 = 8, 5, 12 or 0?

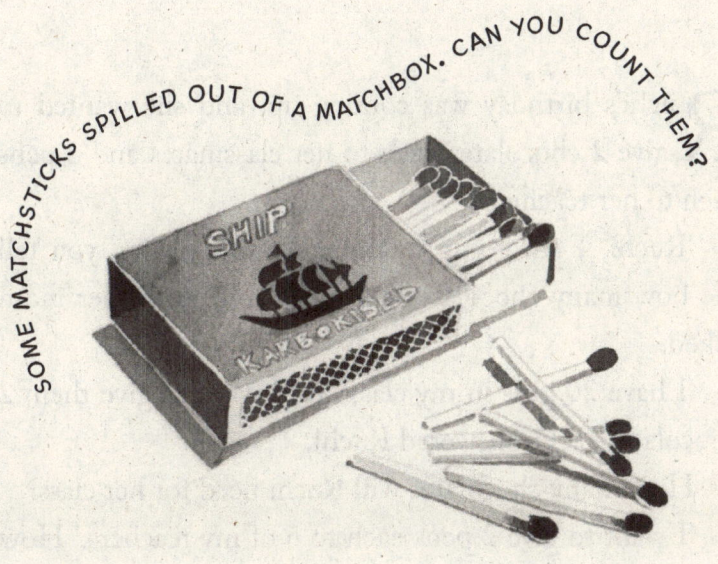

SOME MATCHSTICKS SPILLED OUT OF A MATCHBOX. CAN YOU COUNT THEM?

# Ruchi's Birthday Treat

Ruchi's birthday was coming up, and she wanted to give 2 chocolates each to her classmates and 2 pens each to her teachers.

'Ruchi, I am going to the store today. Can you tell me how many chocolates and pens you need?' her mom asked.

'I have 20 girls in my class and I want to give them 2 chocolates each,' answered Ruchi.

How many chocolates will Ruchi need for her class?

'I want to give 2 pens each to 6 of my teachers.' How many pens in total did Ruchi need for her teachers?

'I also want to give 2 extra sweets each to my 6 best friends,' said Ruchi. How many extra sweets would her mom need to buy?

# Taxi!

Sayoni and Seema lived in neighbouring houses. And they always went everywhere together. On Mondays, they went together to art class and on Wednesdays, for athletics. On Fridays, they went swimming.

Supriya Didi, who accompanied them to class, would flag down a taxi for the three of them. Sayoni and Seema had made a game of it. If they got into a taxi with a registration number that ended with an odd number, Sayoni would get 1 point. If the taxi's registration plate had an even number as its last digit, then Seema would get 1 point.

That week, they got taxis numbered 4451 and 6643 on Monday, 2454 and 5545 on Wednesday, and 3792 and 6353 on Friday. Who got more points?

# Green Thumbs

Gardening class was so much fun! Simmy Aunty took the children to parks and gardens and showed them so many kinds of leaves and flowers and roots. But what Nainika loved the most was planting little saplings and seeds. She loved to get her hands messy and feel the coolness of the soil as she dug into it.

Today, they were growing kitchen herbs. There were 4 children in the class. Each of them had a small rectangular planter filled with soil. They were going to plant different herbs in it.

Nainika was in charge of giving out the mint plants. Simmy Aunty had given her 8 plants. How many plants did Nainika give each child?

Surabhi had 12 basil plants. If every child got the same amount of plants, how many did Surabhi give each of them?

Ahmed was in charge of the lemongrass. He had 20 stalks of the herb. How many stalks of lemongrass did each child get?

Ayaan equally divided 24 seeds of coriander amongst the children. How many seeds did each one get?

The children collected their plants, picked up their small spades and some water, and began work on their planters.

After two minutes of digging, Nainika threw her spade down and ran to hide behind Simmy Aunty. 'Eeeekkk!' she squealed.

And then Ayaan did the same, closely followed by Surabhi.

'What's wrong?' Simmy Aunty and Ahmed asked in unison. 'Look,' said Surabhi, pointing to the planters. Ahmed looked closely at the three planters and only found a tiny earthworm in each! Simmy Aunty had a good laugh.

# Dadaji's Pillbox

Dadaji had to take many pills every day. He had a little box with 7 small compartments in it, 1 for each day of the week. Every Sunday, Sahil helped Dadaji fill the box for the whole week, so he would not forget to take his pills every day.

Dadaji gave Sahil all the pills that he was to take during the week—12 green pills and 7 yellow pills.

Dadaji had to take the green pills on Monday, Wednesday and Friday. Since Dadaji had given Sahil 12 green pills, how many of these did he put in the three compartments meant for Monday, Wednesday and Friday?

And he had to take 7 yellow pills over 7 days. So how many would go into each compartment from Monday to Sunday?

# Animal Love

Tanya loved animals and she often volunteered to feed the abandoned and old animals at the pet shelter near her house.

The shelter, which needed a new kennel, had decided to raise money for it by selling raffle tickets. Tanya was eager to help. She took 50 tickets from them to sell.

First, she decided to go to each flat in her building. There were 8 floors in the building and each floor had 2 flats. How many flats in all could she sell the tickets to?

How many tickets would be left?

Then, she sold tickets to her 4 aunts, 3 uncles, and 2 cousins. How many had she sold to her family?

Her parents had agreed to buy the remaining tickets. How many were left for them to buy?

# The Busy Train

Maya clutched her mother's hand as they boarded the train at the first station—Churchgate.

Every Saturday, Maya and her mom went to Bandra to spend the day with her grandma.

They always took the mid-morning train, because it wasn't that crowded. *Ta-tak ta-tak ta-tak ta-tak*, the local train clattered on the tracks as it sped across the length of Mumbai. Maya eagerly looked out of the window, waiting for the familiar landmarks and stations to appear. They had caught a fast train that would stop at only 5 stations between Churchgate and Bandra:

Churchgate

Marine Lines

Charni Road

Grant Road

Mumbai Central

Dadar

Bandra

At Marine Lines, a lady selling all kinds of hair accessories got into their compartment. She showed Maya neon-coloured hairbands and butterfly clips. And for just Rs 20, she got a bagful of pretty stuff for her hair. How many stops after Churchgate was Marine Lines?

On the second stop after Marine Lines, she knew that the small boy selling colouring books would board the train. At which station did the boy with the colouring books climb into their compartment?

Mumbai Central was a big and busy station. Maya drew back and sat close to her mom, as a huge rush of people got into the train once it came to a halt. How many stops from Churchgate was Mumbai Central? The lady who sold hair accessories got off at this station and always took another train back to Marine Lines. How many stops would she pass on her way back?

After Mumbai Central, how many more stops would Maya and her mom have to pass before they reached Bandra?

# Fair Day

The fairground was bright and noisy. The rides looked so exciting! The Ferris wheel turned round and round like a giant green circle of light. The bumping cars crashed into each other cheerfully. The wooden horses rose up and down on the carousel, while the bungee jump went *zing, zing, zing*, as the children bounced up and down. There was also a toy train that went round a track.

Khadija—who had Rs 100—wanted to make the most of her visit to the fair. She first went for a ride on the Ferris wheel, the carousel and bumping cars, then tried bungee jumping, and finally sat in the toy train. Each of these rides cost Rs 10. How much money had she spent? How much did she have left?

Her friend Paulomi came running to her and said, 'Let's go and get some candyfloss and popcorn!'

'Great idea!' said Khadija. She bought candyfloss for Rs 4 and popcorn for Rs 6. How much did she spend on these goodies?

And they decided they would finish off their treat with an ice cream. Khadija bought 1 for herself and 1 for Paulomi, each of which cost Rs 5. How much did she spend on the ice creams?

Khadija was thrilled that after all the fun she had had, she still had some money left to put into her piggy bank back home. How much did she manage to save?

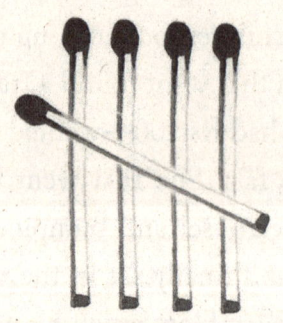

# What Happened to the Horses?

Gallops, a camp where children could learn horseback riding, was situated in a small valley surrounded by rugged hills. The grassy paddocks in the camp were a lovely green and the stables were sturdy with whitewashed walls and tiled roofs.

In these stables were 12 beautiful horses.

Every summer, a group of 24 children attended the camp. And all the horses were brought out of the stable for morning rides. How many students were assigned to each horse?

One morning, Ram Sharan, the stable hand, found out that 4 of the horses had fallen sick. So they were not taken out for the morning ride. How many horses were fit? And how many students were assigned to each horse now?

The next day, 2 more horses fell ill. How many were no longer fit for the morning ride?

Everyone was worried. The staff checked the hay, the feed, the water and all around the paddock, but no one could say what was making the horses sick.

Eleven-year-old Tinaaz and nine-year-old Malika decided to play investigators. That evening after class, they hid themselves in some nearby bushes and watched as the horses were let loose in the paddocks.

They saw a horse walking towards the far end of the field. On taking a closer look, they found a small gap in the fence through which the horse had squeezed himself out. There, he stood grazing. However, the vegetation in this field had been sprayed with a lot of pesticide. So, when the horses ate this grass, they got sick!

The two girls ran to their instructor and told her what they had seen. She quickly brought back the horses that had crossed the fence. The veterinarian then treated the sick horses.

On the final day of the camp, when the children put up a special show for their families, all 12 horses were present, proud to carry their little charges. Everyone clapped for the children as they rode. And guess who got the most cheers?

# Cake Count

Suma's Bakery made the best cakes ever! Eleven-year-old Sanya was spending her summer helping her aunt, Suma—the one who owned the bakery. Sanya's job was to answer the phone and note down the orders.

'Hello! Suma's Bakery,' said Sanya, as she picked up the day's first call. 'Just a minute . . .'

'Suma Maasi, the lady on the phone wants a cake that would be enough for 4 people. How many kilograms should she order?'

'Half a kilogram for 4 people,' answered Suma.

'Ma'am, you will need half a kilogram. Which cake would you like to have?' And so, she wrote down an order for a half a kilogram of chocolate cake.

In the next hour, she took down 3 more orders. Can you tell from each order, how many kilograms the following people had ordered?

Mrs Alphonso—pineapple gateau for 8 people.
Reema Rao—Black Forest for 12 people.
Yumna Syed—almond sponge for 4 people.

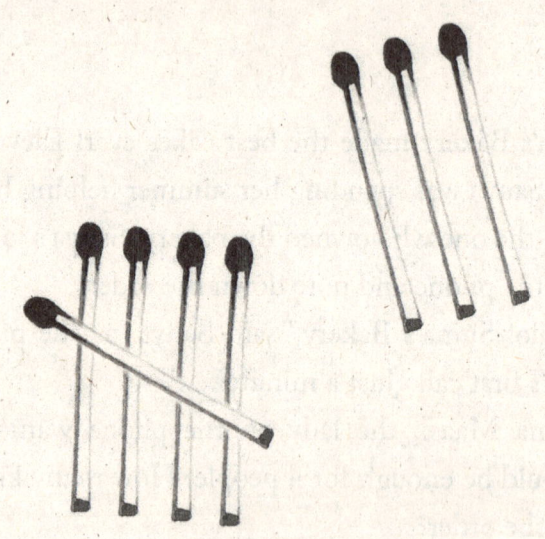

# An Intergalactic War

'Pow, Pow!' Riddhima pointed her space soldiers towards Prithvi's spacecraft. 'I will win this space war!' she said.

'No, I will!' insisted Prithvi.

'I have 3 soldiers in each of my 3 spaceships and 2 soldiers in each of my 12 space pods,' declared Riddhima, challenging him.

'Ha! I have 4 soldiers in each of my 3 spaceships and 12 soldiers in each of my 2 space stations.'

'Oh, you silly people!' said Madhu, Prithvi's elder sister. 'Obviously, it will be a draw!'

Was Madhu right? Did Riddhima and Prithvi have the same number of soldiers?

# Finish the Book!

Tejal and Sanah always had their noses in a book. And every time they went to the school library, they borrowed dozens of books. At the moment, both girls had 1 book each—they hadn't finished reading it, yet they wanted more.

'Oh, no, you two! I will let you borrow more books only after you have finished the ones you already have!' said Ms Manisha, the librarian.

Tejal's book had 180 pages, out of which she had read 155 pages. How many more pages did she have left to finish the book?

Sanah's book had 175 pages, and she had reached page 160. How many pages did she have to read yet?

If Tejal and Sanah read 5 pages each in a day, how many days would they take to finish their respective books?

# One Star More than Mine

On summer nights, Sabina's family spread their mattresses on the terrace and slept in the open. Staring at the night sky, Sabina asked, 'Mom, who owns the stars in the sky?'

Her mom smiled and said, 'I own a 1000 of them.'

'Oh? Do I own any?' Sabina asked.

'Yes,' replied her mother. 'You own as many as I do, plus 1.'

How many stars did Sabina believe she owned?

The next night, Sabina asked her dad, 'How many stars do you own?'

'1005,' replied her dad, smiling.

'Oh, that's more than what I own!' said Sabina.

How many stars more than Sabina did her dad have?

# Splash!

Mia ran to the edge of the pool 5 times and then ran back again each time. She wouldn't step into the water; she was just too scared. This was the tenth day that she had done exactly the same thing. How many times altogether had she tried to get into the pool over these 10 days?

'Come on, Mia!' shouted her friends. So she decided to try one last time. Alas, she couldn't build her courage and turned back, only to bump into a child who was trying to run past her. And . . . splash! Mia fell into the pool! But when she was finally in the water, she found that she liked it very much indeed!

# Are We There yet?

Oh, when was this car journey going to end? The road to the hill station was beautiful, but the journey was taking so long that both Shane and his sister, Theresa, were getting irritated. 'Let's play a game,' said their mother, noticing that they were bored. 'How about a treasure hunt? If you see a cow, you get 10 points; if you see a blue car, you get 20; if you see a horse, you get 40! Whoever sees one of these first will get 10 bonus points. The one who gets the most points will get an extra ice cream when we stop for a break next,' their mother explained.

*Extra ice cream!* Hearing these words, the children stopped complaining and instantly began peering out of the window.

'I saw a cow, I saw a cow!' shouted Theresa.

'No, you didn't!' exclaimed Shane in disbelief.

'Yes, I did! Look, right there on the hill!' crowed Theresa. 'So I get 10 points plus 10 bonus points.'

'Fine!' said Shane, sulking.

And so this went on, with both the children happily spotting cows, blue cars and horses. The journey now seemed to fly by. Just as they drove into town, they saw a hotel.

'Time for ice cream!' announced their father.

'I saw 8 cows, 10 blue cars and 1 horse!' said Shane.

'And I saw 7 cows, 10 blue cars and 1 horse!' said Theresa.

'It seems we have a tie,' said their father. Is it truly a tie? How many points did each of them get?

# Happy Diwali!

Such excitement! Shaila loved getting ready to celebrate Diwali. This year, she had bought a beautiful *ghagra choli* in red and gold, with bangles to match. She was now going to help her mom decorate the house.

Mom was standing on the stepladder and pulling out boxes of lamps from the loft. 'Be careful,' she said, as she passed them down to Shaila. 'Each box has 10 lamps. We need to place 40 lamps in the balcony. How many boxes should I take out?' she asked. What was Shaila's reply?

Then, her mom found the beautiful paper lanterns that they had made the previous year. 'Look, we have a dozen of these. We should put them on all of our 6 doors,' she said. How many could they hang from each door frame?

On the morning of Diwali, the florist delivered garlands of fresh marigold. There were 24 garlands in all. If the garlands were to be used to decorate the same 6 doors, how many garlands could Shaila and her mom decorate each door frame with?

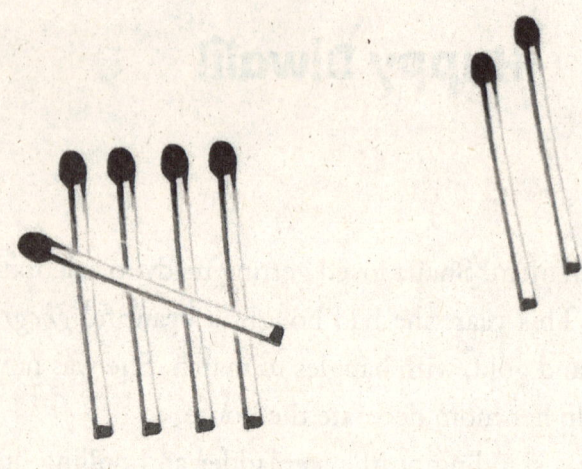

# Uncle Maths

Shayaan loved Wednesdays. That was the day Purab uncle visited. Purab uncle always had so many fun stories and games to share. But the ones Shayaan loved most were his maths games. At the end of each visit, Purab uncle gave him a mega maths challenge. Winning that challenge meant winning a grand prize! Today, his prize was to be a cricket ball autographed by Sachin Tendulkar.

'Okay Shayaan,' said uncle. 'Here is your challenge—you have to divide 25 erasers equally among a few imaginary friends and remember, each friend should get an equal number of erasers.'

So he started with two imaginary friends. However, when he tried to divide 25 by 2, he managed to give 12 to each, but still had 1 left.

Then he divided by 3. Dividing 25 by 3 gave three imaginary friends 8 each. But still, there was 1 left over.

Next he tried by 4 and 5. One of them did in fact win him the prize! Which number was it?

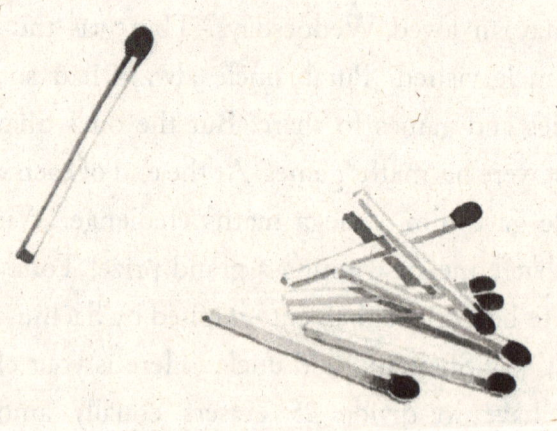

# Ms Bad Temper

Ms Dayal was always in a bad temper. She was always shouting at the class.

'Why haven't you opened your books yet?'

'No talking!'

But the thing she loved to do the most was to cut points from the overall house points.

The children were divided into three houses at school, and depending on their behaviour—good or bad—their house would gain or lose points.

Right now, Red House was leading with 50 points, Green was not far behind with 48 and Blue had 40 points.

The summer holidays were about to begin and the prize for 'best house' would be awarded just before school closed. The students carefully put on their best behaviour, since they did not want to lose any points.

The children were working quietly in class that day, when Ms Dayal walked past Tara and found her fidgeting.

'Tara, stop it at once!' she barked.

'Miss, I think I've lost my eraser,' said Tara, softly.

'You can look for it later.'

'But—'

'Minus 2 for Red House, since you are disturbing the class!'

*Oh no, what will my housemates say!* Tara thought, horrified.

How many points did Red House have now?

As Ms Dayal walked past Mithi's desk, she saw the girl dive under her seat. The girl had just discovered that her sharpener was missing. And so, Green House, to which Mithi belonged, lost 2 points as well. How many points did Green House have now?

The teacher passed by Suraj. His pencil disappeared, so he just sat there, not continuing the classwork!

'What is wrong with all of you today? Blue House, minus 2!' the teacher yelled, noticing the boy. Uh-oh! How many points was Blue House now down to?

Just as Ms Dayal was about to go back to her table, Keval—a chubby, shy fellow—said, 'Miss . . .' But when she looked straight at him, the boy became tongue-tied!

'Keval! If you don't speak up, I will cut points from your house too!' Ms Dayal threatened.

Keval was terrified, but he had to speak. 'Miss, your dupatta,' he managed to whisper.

'What is it?' she asked him angrily, as she lifted the ends of her dupatta to inspect it.

And lo and behold, entangled in the loose threads of her dupatta were the missing eraser, sharpener and pencil. The objects had got caught in the fabric as Ms Dayal had swept past the children's desks.

Luckily, Ms Dayal did have a sense of humour. She burst out laughing, and the entire class joined in too.

Keval, who had hidden his face in embarrassment, was only too thrilled to hear the otherwise ill-tempered teacher say, 'Plus 5 to all the houses to make up for my mistake. And an extra 5 points to Keval's Blue House for speaking up for his friends.'

'Hurrah!' shouted the class. How many points did each house have? Which house was now leading?